UNFINISHING

unfinishing

BRIAN HENDERSON

McGill-Queen's University Press
Montreal & Kingston • London • Chicago

ISBN 978-0-2280-1149-1 (paper)
ISBN 978-0-2280-1291-7 (ePDF)
ISBN 978-0-2280-1292-4 (ePUB)

Legal deposit second quarter 2022
Bibliothèque nationale du Québec

Printed in Canada on acid-free paper that is 100% ancient forest free
(100% post-consumer recycled), processed chlorine free

Funded by the Government of Canada   Financé par le gouvernement du Canada   Canada   Canada Council for the Arts   Conseil des arts du Canada

We acknowledge the support of the Canada Council for the Arts.

Nous remercions le Conseil des arts du Canada de son soutien.

Library and Archives Canada Cataloguing in Publication

Title: Unfinishing/Brian Henderson.

Names: Henderson, Brian, 1948– author.

Series: Hugh MacLennan poetry series.

Description: Series statement: The Hugh MacLennan poetry series |
  Poems.

Identifiers: Canadiana (print) 20210382090 | Canadiana (ebook)
  20210382120 | ISBN 9780228011491 (softcover) |
  ISBN 9780228012917 (PDF) | ISBN 9780228012924 (ePUB)

Classification: LCC PS8565.E51 U54 2022 | DDC C811/.6—dc23

This book was typeset by Marquis Interscript in 9.5/13 Sabon.

For Charlene, heart of my life

There is no perception ... not permeated with memories.
Henri Bergson, *Matter and Memory*

Time ... is a fire which consumes me, but I am the fire ...
a world made of time ... a tireless labyrinth, a chaos, a dream.
Jorge Luis Borges, *A New Refutation of Time*

CONTENTS

fortune teller

present perfect

PROLEPSIS

ANICCA A JAN-KEN

made out of paper made
                    out of stone
of rock scissors made out of paper
of shredded time stored in me
memory and counter-memory
made out of
                    lightning flicker
yellow-shafted red-headed rose-breasted
                    water clock
made out of storm cloud
the afterthought of thunder
of a garden gate banging in the wind
out of a shroud neck-bruise
nighthawks swifts
                    passenger pigeons
of anguish loss failed attention lists
                    impatience
out of elemental joy
the shadow of a falcon's streaming flight
out of accidents apocrypha dream residue
                    out of ever again
out of scissors
paper vibrational sand
                    unmoored stone boats
raft of floating doors
because what's inside you
                    is outside you

a place
where you can move both forward
and backward
                              in a single motion
trying to find out how to be here
made out of air and waves
the many kinds of winged people
                              out of
the candelabra descending
straight out of the wall
its horizontal flames
paper scissor rock
made out of truth and consequences
the singing bowl of these poems
                              resting on their edges
having come a long way in the night
made out of

VANISHING HOUSES

APRANIHITA

or maybe

the continuing story of ending

        the end

or maybe the strangeness

of knowledge
wasted on knowing

thrown out the window of the passing
dictionary train prison window

instead there is the kintsugi of this broken vase
in which the Phalaenopsis
bloomed for months

there is the moment of what you thought was failure

there is the falling that becomes flight

how many wishes are these

at the bottom of the lake a rainbow of silt forms
invisible except to those who have forgotten how to swim

and here along the silence of the valley of clouds
stories disperse

but everything is anyway
both always different
from its selves
and still themselves anyway

nearly weightless smears of time

VANISHING HOUSES

(after Lev Vygotsky)

condensed inner speech that
doesn't speak but is there

no words but linguistic arrival holes

Dermisache loops you fall through the

doors of and the fall of
behind you

those vanishing houses
the ones floating away on the flood
the drowned ones
those burnt
those buried in the avalanche
those whose doors could not be held closed
those dreamed and lived in
the ones the light married to the darkness

is how you got here

LOBELIA CARDINALIS

unblessed they nonetheless bloom in the wetlands beyond strife

they take up the discarded feathers of cardinals
    and transform them
into inflorescence
which is why you seldom find the feathers

in a language with its teeth on fire and intermittent
birthdays of unequally spelled names
they recite their heart sutras

the intricate shutters of their blood cameras
open and close on us
as we walk through the bog and on
the deer who pass and the deer flies
bees dragonflies garter snakes porcupine elm
aspen ash maple cedar song sparrows
redwings waxwings cattail lady's slipper and

at night they turn the record of these various passages into scores

for the small ringing oblivion of tree frog orchestras

who would have imagined beginnings themselves
would have no beginning

when we slip into our skins it's like water feldspar winking
with its many mica eyes

we imbibe small tassels of time

who can follow the thread as it's weaving
in and out of the traffic of the body

someone is moving the words around when we sleep
perhaps a fisher or hare

perhaps the arms of trees shrugged when in the evening
we found the river had slithered away under a rock

we can hear its dry tongue whispering we can hear
music of ghostlight harrowing the margins of beech leaves

we can see geese hauling the boat of the moon
out of the trees where it's been sleeping

and hear them pulling this knot that's us
inside out

this one
and
this

glide of dragonfly
over mirror water

pine shining
like a blizzard

stairs steep
taking two at a time

the tiny black and white tiles

arms and fingers spread
flying back down

the one thing
you could speak then
had nothing
to do with anything

that second between
when a door is locked
and a window blows open

and through which one thing
after another
escapes

PHANTOMANCY

wooden chatterboxes of
steamer trunks whirlybirds
two chairs with wings
a small St James
a White Owl box
with badges medals
not exactly tabulae rasae but maybe
things hidden on eternal table lands
once upon a time
or a card table I can fold down into the pluperfect
future progressive maybe
where slow yellow bullets of bees still flare
in the dark ambush of garden using up
all their beauty

but what else should they do with it
the scattered stones
still memorizing time also have something to say
the river glamoured with lightning's
hungry rivers
and dusk once
a pentimento
on the back door of the word

if the first language was stars and the second air

you can cut yourself on a phantom of water
a letter a river a simple beginning or even a moment
of near recognition earth
flying up over the sun

and feel my life's been descending into me all this time
what is it in the morning the me is

when I wake up and give thanks
for what's left
of the world

twist torque loop return

just as we begin
to get inside things they turn inside out
and you have to love that moment

when the flight of language touches down in you

sleep's another

matchbox event horizon rapids

bigger on the inside
some things can teach us how to be

but only now
am I beginning to think sufficiently sideways

a sideways glance in the mirror that reveals
nothing

maybe some reeds
a stairway of wings

AFTER ALL THIS TIME

I may have burned out
        places
yet to re-visit
                the house
collapsing to the west   as clouds pour off the roof
eastward   and stillness
         crashes over us
                    like a sea
burned up burned over burned down
places I only vaguely remember existed
                    and maybe because
it's only a would-be guide
                      this idea of one truthful
   moment

we are what we tell ourselves
so everyone is
        losing something

the body a mere practitioner of time

in the visible world

this clatter this pull into the noise of things into
                    that
void   that
        silence
if the   [abandoned]
poem   speaks

in the visible world
what you find
you may be able

               to write down

but why

               do we need

        to
need

                                what

  we have forgotten
        remembers us
               the quality of light
is always changing   without words
clouds   drifting   through
           glass

TEXTS (AT THE END OF THE WORLD)

pre-text
con-
text
across dry land
stream script
written through rock
seen from 1,000 feet up
cirrus arcs miles higher
pull and draw
weave of rock
and sand

burnt-over scrub
and pine
not default choice
architectures
but a long way from rain

and found
in the writing
this illegibility
of what I used to think
I could easily
read

but what's this
a nearly perfectly good leather recliner
in the middle of the burnt-out Sierra

maybe I'll just sit here a moment
and see if I can spy
a floating hieroglyph

a near-to-last condor

there

or is it
floating ash

your wings
your number tag

ache of the arc
of that flight

a spectre a speculation weaving high
over the would-be stabilizing apparatuses
and the charred earth

this smoke
a messenger
urtext

once upon a time the years move across our garden
like shadows of stratocumulus candles
burn down into wells of ·themselves

the heron a hungry philosopher in blue
pretends indifference at the goldfish pond
when we look again
many small lives have vanished
and the heron too

we imagine him rowing into the heavy sky
disturbed by slivers of gold-red thought
and maybe it's a kind of love

there's also the love of light for water
of rain for earth that falls
into its waiting arms the mirror's
sheer sheet of water
for its images the book for its
one true reader the secret cave of night
for the brazen fleet of clouds of dawn
my brain for the smell of you
tongue for the red unfolding root of your heart

the pond that gets overwritten in a script of ice in winter
when snow nearly plunges the stream into silence
breeds again its small gold bells of frog throats its shiny fish

here unlike elsewhere time unlike mercury
or lead does not accumulate but sheds
its skin throws its seeds molts melts
and from a worn stone a fallen primary
or the small bleached vertebrae of a goldfish
from these thrown and exuberantly
tossed-aside things begins again

SO THIS IS WHAT IT WAS LIKE

having a piece of the night draped
across his body
her breast a moon against his left shoulder

when she got up to pee he could hear the clock
a hand-wound type that after a few days
of concentrating on its task
loses focus and begins thinking about other things
perhaps the fugue of souls

when he woke it was half past the early light
washing out any stars and so still in the room
he could hear the slightest movement an eye
opening or the dreamed deciding not to waken the dreamer

COMBERS

coming home there is one knife
curating the kitchen
the comma of a bird's beak knife
on the island
and me in my coma the tide
sliding in
someone tells me time
bounces off the sun
and if reason will not answer time
might

why then is the trigger so happy
when even in the fog we have at least a few seconds

sometimes I feel as though
I'm not anywhere close to myself

this poem faltering
its way to you

I'm ashamed of being
the empty one

still
       in this noisescape
with its disingenuous waterbird people
and misaligned temples
its crisscrossed combers
fog horns slowly sculpt
their rhythmic thinking
in shrouds of mist
through which the whispers
of our breathing slide

ON WHAT IS IN THE FIRST PLACE

there's the poetry that says it's late
you'd think I'd have learned something by now
there's the poetry of code and of prayer
there's poetry of estrangement and of comfort
of hijinks and of ceremonial celebration
cerebral transmigration machine
hunger dictation spiritnoise the moment
I no longer know or know only far beneath something else
and it's possible I needed to forget whatever it is or was
if I ever knew it in the first place

and what is in the first place

not a rope of time a glint a knot
implicating things in all directions weave of light on water water
braided in evening September light wing-surging
air pumped from wefting flights
of geese so close overhead having
shed all their reflections into the lake's scattering
the haptic cardiograph of their calling

soon they'll return for those truths about themselves
but even in so short a time
those will have drifted under the floor of the lake
only to unfold as if for the first time
on their splashed arrival

INTERFERENCE PATTERNS

falls

one small bead splashing

into your hand

in the rear-view mirror

the past comes accelerating

lights blaring something

breaks

and spins away backward

off the wing

of memory

was there a garden

poppies peonies

by the river of the afterlife

three sharp knocks

waking me

from my dream

but no one at my door

nor anyone anywhere to be seen

the reefed moon

heeled over on a broad reach

driving N by NW

towards the underworld's recurrent

calling

INTERFEROMETER

what are the chances to the mystery
and otherness and beauty of the world
the timeline wavering a black comet just responding in turn
with something beautiful &

strange assemblages interference
patterns objects custodians
of our narratives he said (Peter Schwenger that is) but
they are also their own interferometers in the wilderness
of consciousness metering
interbeing and alterity

for instance maybe time's door-mirrors
where you enter the who you see
the thought you might
carry even the echoes of twisted
ideologies pro terra nullius market
QA bodycamless patria drone entitlement
steeped in the rising of the seas and endless
recurring fires but
you find yourself luckily slowing
to a stop
here

because fingernails of ice have been tapping at the winter
    window

because humility means of the earth
where everything begins

surrounded by the thinking of trees the surf
roaring in their outstretched hands of sky of clouds of light
of falling waves of light and the slow thinking of trees in winter
no slower than my own than the waves of snow
the staccato sharp waves of the calls of a jay
each one a point in time

did I mention water probably
not since it's frozen what is
a stopped even if momentarily
wave

walking the coastline in a photo
poised April omen of a hummingbird
this daydream each letter holding its breath
a little perforation through the page of the world

though not heavy they fall nonetheless
burned-off fragments of a life that.tear these holes in sleep
     you know
time crystals excoriated by the breeze

the answers have nothing in them the pictures
are of whom why is the landscape
the maple and beech hills aspen wetlands
you can see from the height of the deck
moving

while the sky's evening
peach-light-lit
cloud-temples
are
motionless
suspended

forever over the archeology of now

MUTAGENIC

clatter of halyards in the cross-breeze
of horizontal inheritance the poem

is a mutagen
or the words in it

mute again the deadly solvents
used to extract one small lithium
syllable

I let the long wave roll out
capsizing all the smallcraft
in the harbour of my thinking swamping
every thought every memory
foundered

like shaking all the crumbs candles pens
and books off the bed in a single
heave of the sheet
like standing in an earthwave
irradiated at anchor
riding out the labyrinthine seductions of childhood

swans the dead the longed-for
answers I could have taken
a detour here
along the crest and
descended into the valley where the spatterdock
docks every Wednesday with its stolen mail
but got blown slightly
off course

BENT WATER LIGHT SOMETHING

beholds
Nothing that is not there and the nothing that is

there is a kind of shade-ripple

there is a déjà sense everywhere and I am standing here
at the window immersed in it

dream-like bent water-light or something like the sound
I'd once known by heart but have since long forgotten
a gate banging in the deepening dusk

someone a boy sitting in a chair at the water's edge
a mile away in the ruined glimmer
with his head in his hand

me or maybe someone else's memory I've brushed against
an edge-glimmer of which there is memory but no edge jamais

no one no gate no glimmer but the feel of that glimmering
though there is nothing here

before anything being remembered
sliding away coming into being

there is just memory-ness

and if by luck I happen to return to my own life now
how would I recognize it

HOLD THE PHONE

I'll just put the phone down for a sec
the elaborate brook and waterfall
of grosbeak song spills
thru afternoon light
what if I said I'm trying to live
one life at a time
I've been pretending so long
is this a temple of leaves
look at this spiral
nights I'm studying neurocosmology
so the moment I turned the wheel
the accident in which I nearly killed us
was waiting for me right there
and so in fact I'll just hang up
and maybe try my call again later

ON AFTERLIVES

stars' clocks faintly counting backwards

the world is flat and folded

a fleet of crows
silently dipping their black oars in air

is it the deceased or the living
who continue

at the point of death

each using their own lost things
as fuel

VEILED THROUGH REVELATION

(after Carel Willink)

glint in the open the tall window with its wall of cloud

shark-gill sky city resting on its glissando canals

I would have loved the water its cupped hands

the consulate of dreams as it lets one of its dreamers go

at the edge of belief into the starvation of steep blue

the home current

floating gilled and gilded parachutes

even beauty's ferocity a squeeze of light

under the eyelid

the dreamer crawling through

iron gates swung open

into the arms of these words

tiny glass antiques mineral lives
with outspoken secrets folded like linen
or clouds
mapping the lands of silence druzied
with light and wind it somehow flows but is still
there every cell a well
in long tendrils rain ribbons in fact
you have to forget what you're looking for
to have a chance of finding it

did it seep up from the inflamed core or
pour down in the 700-million-year bombardment vapoured
　　words

but the water-bridge is a glitter-shower falling into the gorge
when you find yourself sitting on the curb
wondering what just happened amid wordsparks and traffic
a deciduous consecration of glass particles the river
of a streetcar washing through you

and someone there in the park smiling kindly

you take a photograph with the word personally
and erase it
that would be what water would say
because everything is too close and too far away at once
and you go down to the creek to listen to it saying it
over and over

of sleep the crackle
flicker
hiss
the nerve noise flickering
a fire in the woods of the body
on the tangle of lightless
wordstairs rhizomic coruscations
rising memory trolling

with spiky spoons
awake to the night's splinters
along the blood ink river
wading barefoot in the shallows
you look up the hill

two small candles of fall
maples in the dark cedars

I cannot tell the difference
between looking and dreaming
between the living and the dead

on either side of this darkness
the children running on the beach at dusk
the purple baseball cap
the folkboat wing-and-wing
the waterlogged log sailing
through the air toward the boy's skull

neither can I tell what here is
speaking exactly
in its scratched-out narrative
at 4:30 in the morning

everything absent
despite not having been taken away

water opening her hands

the architecture of falling

snow stars the speech of leaves

love vertigo melodies

bond rates bombs

these congeries

below the threshold

of everything

is everything

and saying partakes of this

falling

and then re-

reading this message

sent you just now I fail

to recognize

the phrases of

and when read again

are different again

and yet again yet again

fall completely

through recognition

the message re-

inventing its phrases

every time I read

the flashzone of panic

each word turning

its light toward me

and then flashing out

a trap door

through which I fall

which then springs back into place

to reveal another

through which I keep

falling

and

MORE MISUNDERSTANDINGS

how many
misunderstandings
can one life
be based on

perhaps just one

fountain of ink
or deep caves of clouds
you thought you knew

the you
you were
and if you are

but a spectator
why are you not
observing

the closing
of the very first animal

the parliament of dragonflies
passing a law
rendering humans Hippoboscidae

and when I asked for help
they said
join a basketball team

a long train
of immunizations

horses
leaping
from the carousel

the last living elms
tossing
their still heavy manes

each facet
of your eye
a sky
moving backwards

there was more
compassion
in the stone
than in all the shale
of these words

so now might be a good time
to learn how to sit in a room
with silence

now that the island
has drifted further downwind

now that the breathing
of the elevators
has nearly stopped

now that a door of light
has drifted through the wall
as the name of an ancestor

and after months of wandering
in the valleys
of the tuning forks

each answer a machine
for hiding things

and the rain
the rain in falling

falls as if falling
might save it

whatever I was I am
no longer my life
a box of locked padlocks
from the old community mailbox
they've replaced by the lake

I'm writing on stone paper
I'm sitting on the couch
the couch is grey and is made
for sitting and writing
it can be quite comfortable

except that beside me
sit the unwritten
the tide sliding in on the
shingle at my feet
water looking under every stone

the spinnaker of moon
pulling me west
gulls wheeling high
their minds extending

all the way to wingtip
in the nearly empty

courtroom the glow of dust motes
wood
railings desks chairs
disembodied
calm as if in a photograph

in fact stone paper can be recycled
but only in a separate process
rematerialized
I haven't given up

sheets of rain
wind tides
everyone's life a spell

evening slides out of the envelope of sky
its invitation to the casino of stars

each with its own signature ministry
of whispers resonant
cell assembly each
photon a photograph the hallucinatory
trance of history the other

world entangled with this one at every
point and every point a threshold it's not
clear which or which has forgotten
its belonging to which and the familiar
beings the pure remoteness of presence

you walk out into the sensorium of
luminescence the darkness lets you see
the moon's whetstone there sharpening
the blindsight of luck

where the thinking that starts from nowhere
begins

I'M TALKING TO YOU TONIGHT
FROM RADIO NOWHERE

you are listening this evening to radio nowhere
the stars snap in their clarity
and the smoke rolls over the hills like mist
a squadron of pelicans skims the wavetops of your eyelids
picking up the darkness of the last living light
and
what have you been
standing there
waiting for
ears rushed with silence
wind streaming you out on the tether of night
a shadow cast backward
by the future

FORTUNE TELLER

A KEY IN THE SHAPE OF A KITE

debris will have been harbouring secrets
                                        a key in the shape of
    a kite

thirsty
out of an old rain barrel you will scoop language
read Harappan
                                        channel Martian

what is in you will be more than you

the stone will look at you and see sand

and your shopping cart will have been filling with sand

and you will be dining at the water table
                                        looking up elements
periodically

and here is someone who doesn't know about barricades
    about taking a breath or a Valium
someone someone will call security about

but who will listen for the small true voice
who will hear the small true voice

this future is paradox nomenclatures that sleep has not yet
    completely abandoned

here's where you are on the Akashic Record label of the
  polluted rivers

and even though you're not
                                          it will appear as
    though you still are

here's where prophecy is the discovery of the present

and you could go on
                                          but what would you say

neither this
nor that

because you will know less than when you began

where you will open scissors and find mail

the house in whose attic a girl has just been kissing you
                                          as her parents drive up
    the drive

headlights splashing on the rafters

and you will be there still and completely timeless

and that simple event will ask you how
                                          over where you are now
do you understand yourself

have you let go the string

DWELLING

wood

which for you will be not body

but scattered

sparks

green fire of phloem
just beneath your skin

burns its lives

fine slivers of light sharpening the surfaces

the pilot light of the brain

or water

which stands in the fields like mirrors

where we can see the animals we are

slipping into their

mindsets fierce with
crushed ice of stars

which is a cabinet of compelling arguments for lost causes

burning up your idea of lost

and centrifuge

which will be a book that opens worlds to the one who reads it
in total darkness

                                in love
with the slide the burn the spill the curve of the feeling
                        you become

which will be an experiment in separating the self from
    its versions

the closer one of you is to the edge the faster you will travel
and the farther you travel the more sex you will need
                                and the wheel will be
    radiant

        thixotropy

where you become fluid when agitated
                                worried about keeping
    your place in line
a blockchain flowing in one direction only on cryptographic
    hashes

where fluids of brain spine and sex churn the popsicle sticks
    of thinking down the ice and snow melt ditches to where

if you live on the coast
                                the ocean will be coming
    back for you

and if you believe in the last resort
                        you may at least for
    a time
                                            float

EXPECT BILOCATION

slow memory rapids

                                        come close
nearly to be grasped

bestowing the machine whispering of ancient insect choirs
                                        through a quartz keyhole

cascading of tiny parachutes
                                        at the back of the
    mind the sun-twisted houses

whose attics blown off course have begun to be washed
    into sandbars

half-open door
                                        throwing a blade
    of shadow

but even though you might dredge and sift a lifetime it's
    unlikely you'll find what you're looking for
                                        since it's in your other life

the one scribbled by the light looping off the other lake in the
    other house
                                        shadow archive

and this is what it will be like

sleep locked in a room a million light-years away

you will have the eye of anguish and will be

                                       beaten with sticks

you will be tied to the flying carpet

                              the stone of time in
   your pocket

the highway will be closed and you'll be flying
just a few feet over it too fast
when something bursts out of the wet as big as a barred owl

a memory you don't recognize

someone else's who's been here before you and left it behind
   in this other world

open cross-wired non-symbolic

and then once you will have been running with this music
                             it will take you out
   of yourself

repetitive task automation chant

haunt collapse looking for a grace note

and the bird trapped in the house
                           will escape up the
   chimney and you'll stop

right where the dreamer decides not to waken the dreamed

KNOCKING

confession of stones in the interrogation of freeze and thaw
each spring your hands are date stamped
and you will try to twist these stories into answers
and you will have forgotten about invention
made of infinitely cumulative silence
drawn from the steep noise of the earth
you thought you once could hear

now that everything's no longer within reach
you have to change how you dream
truth serum for the confused
jagged as the shards of all the broken glass

in departure might there be a need to knock
and in fact every one of the stones is a door
through which the body of your mind might pass
maybe the one to the house that's no longer there

because rock wants to keep its few remaining watery and
    fiery animals its long dreaming
and you have to knock for some time on those shadows for
    a life to open

they come flying out from under your expectations
and once opened it is rain
and thinking a sandbar
always inventing a different script
never where you left it

and now that the elements are changing places
the fire that burned everything down is as light as air
your memory won't lie down in
night air the constellations of skin shine
and the pain you thought you'd left outside you find in
    your pockets
easily examined at leisure

but there is no need to knock at the door of water or fire
and so a place comes to be called home

NO HESITATION

here's our future
under the clatter of bones thoughts errors scoops
whoops this one can't be ours

iridescent anguishes locked inside a word or some other
    dispensation

though these lives are all we'll ever have
we seem to want to burn them up like kindling
for whose fire

bats turning the evening into a dance floor

ok here's another
            have you ever committed, ordered, incited, assisted,
    or otherwise participated in torture

don't start
if you don't start you'll never stop

            have you committed, ordered, incited, assisted, or
    otherwise participated in extrajudicial killings, political
    killings, or other acts of violence

because if you have you're welcome in the United States
just put your words arranged in small pyres here on the coffin
    table before you go in

there will be alkaloids implanted in the stock exchange
there will be augmented truths
in futures of all kinds
for workers everywhere democracy
having been a passing phase
for beauty is an arrangement of microphones microphytes
    microtines microclines micrographs or microbes
so long as it's understood no one is doing the arrangement
for I am a dead man talking
still wearing the gas the oxygen and the plague mask

let's begin again
with this damnific software
your device will be added to our botnet using the malware
and you can edit your own gene bursts
with a sudden moment of comprehension
with the hieroglyphics of wind spilling off the wings of geese
on their September rehearsal runs
for the wind flows clearer than the mind

the vastness of worlds obscured by the infinite detail of
    finite things
it's what happens next
forget the effing algorithms
jump to where vestigial music crenellates the air
there's no threshold no slice
each minute a thousand inflections of light
when you lie in bed thinking for hours how to get up

when you gently place your hands on her shoulders
you'll need all the extravagant thoughts you just lost
or none at all
a sieve of skin to spill through
the clairvoyance of plants
this apophenia
often the only way to understand how you're alive
reroutes even the terrors of childhood dreams
and waking might finally be within reach
as music falling from the sky like space debris

what then a future
but the practice of memory
and how you turn it inside out
and its insect noise sleeve

it's a fortune
but what exactly is a fortune
but a journey through the present
but an escalation of nerves full of salvage and ornaments
    cascading
one vast song into another
that unstruck
sound sound
of sounds

ENTHEOGEN

this is where it all begins
you could be the one who pretended to be who you were
                              blink don't blink
and found out differently
                    be prepared

fast-forward crashes

into the kairos of the evening's absolute stillness
the flip-side of elm leaves flooded with yellow-shafted
   flicker-light

you could find both star and instar
                              all 22 novels in fact
you could detonate singular moments of lift-off

but truths are reversible
                         your life a palindrome
dromedary in a land where water runs uphill
so thirst might not be your first obligation

                              you might be an edge runner
in the sleep of the moment where the moment
                         of your awakening flows
in fact some of these moments
                         have no moments
because it might not even be you

on the other hand
maybe it's where words reach out to try to understand you
answering the phone in the negative just for some levitation

the tiny fire of hummingbird suspended in midair
hello hello hello looking you in the face
assessing your capacity for high-speed comprehension
what does the real life look like

because all answers can only be incomplete

PHASE CONJUGATION MIRROR

every day will be broken with possible exceptions
possible undercloud downpour light

possible bright darkened flashing seconds partial seconds

dipper flicker kite comma
touch-me-not crescent pearl

redstart foxglove question mark
lady's slipper doll's eyes self-heal

I will begin taking care of my life
right after this
as the place rains straight down into me

when the light collapses under a storm cloud
spattering skeletal Radiolaria
the map of the nowhere from which you've travelled is precise
but you still have to navigate by instinct

for instance cicadas
translating the sounds of their underworld sleep to the opening
    of August
writing out the tripwires of darkness as a kind of celebration

perhaps we'll know one day there wasn't any art
only medicine

me a threshold through which things pass
you a precipice where things stop or soar

your skin the edge of the world in a mime's dream
food for my hands
ventriloquism
syllables of the Pleiades burning up

UNFINISHING

there is an imagining place
and there are places imagined
there is a room with a desk
there on the desk an unopened envelope

I am walking away from a desk
in a house made of envelopes
in a forest made of grasses

where did that hummingbird go

I find myself a stranger
standing in a pool of perfume pouring from the violet-black
   the red petunias
nothing is a mirror

but walking from a future you thought you may have had
   is finding footing
there are over 270 cloud languages in a single raindrop
each one imagining a future
not stories but songs

each step its own downpour its own fragrance
resin rosin raisin reason ricin allowing everything its coming
   and going
spring building its pyramid of light within you

through aerial boundaries perhaps in Sanskrit
the twilight that language is
is the sacred spill of the erotic
is a wild grapevine in the forest

if time does not in fact exist what is it that happens to us
gravity listening to the happiness made out of vanishing as
    it opens and ripples
nothing

is a mirror

PRESENT PERFECT

SUNYATA OR THE REASON WE THOUGHT
THINGS WERE HAPPENING

isn't the reason

and what feels
true
is even less reliable

whose memories for instance

are these that have been stacking up against the fence

someone
kneeling amongst the purple abandonment of delphinium
fluid blood-light leaking out of an ear
turning ever
so slowly the pages of a picture book in the dark

someone not seen
touching another on the shoulder
looking across the lake's chipped slate to the lighthouse
its measured rotation
rotation
rotation of light

I might've been in many places at once
but the garden knows better

on my knees
my hands are in the earth

but when a sly rain begins its slanting through me
looking for something
riffling the pages

what is it

if I say I know

I know

KEY OF MOONLIGHT

I go to a hotel with a river in it

and three rooms completely empty

in which boomerangs made of arms

fling themselves off the walls and hover

shining shops selling gewgaws and gimcracks

to the hive of convention goers

flooding the foyers

in the estuary the river feeds

a train has rammed the shore and lies

crumpled and derailed

I walk the partially submerged cars looking

for a key of moonlight

NIGHTVISION

in the dark room

a word

unvoiced

extends all the way
to the river

and time
that has no scale

is alive in the room

when a moment
plunges into you

it might send you
to where long smoke plumes of snow
ghost off distant cedars

or to where an abandoned rowboat drifts
downstream in the dusk
oars unshipped

or clatter to the floor
in a heap of broken furniture

you would like to be
at the centre of your own life
but there is no such thing
or at least there's no evidence for it or
you're not wearing the right equipment

so you are looking deep into that room

at a sky
with moonlit cloud fishhooks
where remembered things
are imagined

by the currents of the forgotten

and you want to understand something
to hold it longer
than a few seconds or

what luxury

minutes

but everything
brightens

brightens and goes out

as you step into the offworld

IN THE OBLIVION WORLD

of snow
two squall ravens
are streaks of emptiness

asemic climb stall swoop and glide
celebrating their double nonexistence

you tell yourself it's a moment of transition

a revolutionary blizzard
of torn treaties treatises contracts
licences receipts forms and scripts
scriptures manuals news items and yes possibly even
    constitutions

but I seem already to have forgotten the ravens

can you even have second thoughts in utopia

anthracite kites of the gods in a blind torrent

whirled white-out white water
the dead imagining us

cursive
déjà rêvé

TRANCE ACCUMULATION

off snow late-afternoon light
brightens and tarnishes
the walnut face of the wall clock stopped

many years now in its meditation on time

pendulum a small clouded sun in the sky of its trance

as it hunkers into the essence of it

not eyes hair skin
words caresses

but the woods filling up with snow
juncos scotch pine evening

coming on like noteless measureless music
the moments we think of as being

on the other side of it are its revelation

intensities that seem to force fissures in it

a word or two that cannot be said

in a place that has many names you feel it gathering
like gravity along your limbs

and then one day

feathering off your nerves

the way fire feathers wood

COMMEMORATIVE

all it is
is
nothing
more

but
the intensity of feeling

wonder
widely
dispersed

a sentence
drifted
in

everything
that might have been

hovering
in the inward
eye

and here we are
remembering
what it is
that might transpire

leading to the cloud
of its erasure

leaving behind
innumerable invisible impressions
of body-shaped presences

but rarely if ever
what day it was

SPEECHLESS

no hummingbird at the feeder since equinox
but philosophy begins said Wittgenstein
when language goes on holiday
even at summer's end
as the timecurve carves away from you
the words are waving goodbye
zipping past you like a hail of darts
and one of them strikes a human feeling directly
and one of them stops to look you in the face
and then they're gone
and you're speechless

on the ocean of silence
only the raft of my listening

sliding across the hissing fetch
of neurons

water spiders inscribe their self-
erasing scripts

a cardinal depth-sounds
with three single notes

absolute

stillness

there is no time

I seem to remember
a flurry of finches

flight paths but

there is no

time no traffic no clatter even
of agricultural machinery asleep

still in what they still
imagine is what was once called winter

what then
can be
a boundary

I'm hearing the still
sharp light
of burned-out stars

I'm pulling on my plague mask
in diffused dusk

under long spears of cloud
and perhaps I am still

but let's not trouble ourselves too much about nothing
a friend was surprised at passing calculus because she didn't
   think it existed

and an acquaintance tells us of his seven-year-old
   daughter's knack
for discovering large happy numbers and perhaps
the half-life of calculation

in Herzog's book *Conquest of the Useless* a joke is told in which
someone asks a lumberjack looking for work where he'd
   worked last
in the Sahara he replies
but there're no trees there
not any more

you pick up the phone and no one answers
you swear you heard it ringing

the ohm of the mind the imagination of things

ON LOSING AND FINDING

on the walls of thunder lightning's sudden graffiti

beauty the flip side of something estranged

don't take that you can't read it too seriously
things happening at once are happening in different times

happened things
happen now

a fathom down in the golden knot of serpents
the sun ties through the blue of the lake my lost glasses
sun licking wet skin when you raise your arm in an arc
shattering light all around
look what I found

the tractor abandoned in a rocky field in 1948 now
engulfed in whisperings
of aspen and maple

we've been gazing from the height of Montserrat
peering into the wavering distance of the south
where we must have left
the anarchic city of Barcelona to think itself free of hierarchies

fathers first
then mothers
leaving us one by one behind
first one child then another
and another

but this is only ink
one ink or substitute for ink
and things are too readily lost
which unfailingly I used to do

and still do losing
your credit card
in a yellow parking lot or a blue
and in the midst of my self-recrimination fit
you calmly cancel the card
yeah of course

everything drifts downwind leaving
a trail of stars and the distant aspen hill
returned from oblivion

I look up from
this wordscape
to find you

CATECHISM

sometimes I confess I open the pages at random

and finding the first words let them tell me
but how can this be something

about my own life geomancy song paths

may follow the course of bird flight

meander alongside creeks afterwards

I felt as if I were a different person several different
I don't feel it's even me but a whole world

voices gone reflections yes

I've heard the voices down along the river somewhere

a man's voice and a woman's voice calling

I think I saw the river

rippling through the bedroom window shutters waver

of light of air like water your body

a sandbar under this wavering lazy gold

lines edges flaring with rainbow memory
writing themselves out on you

I follow them with my finger follow them follow them
as in another life
rewriting what I would know by heart

WHAT THE DEER KNOW

along the fence line

or what was once

fence line now a colony of aspen stuffing their golden

messages into the blue hat of sky

how can anything hold such clarity

and here someone's old tree fort with a lectern look

but in truth a deer blind luckily unused

the deer having long since learned how to fly

through the unwanted attention of bullets

something I wish they might one day impart to me

stillness

is fragile memory is everywhere only it's not

mine and I know almost nothing of the things that will happen
in some future

though they are here all around me

exhibiting incredible patience among the spent

soot-brown fireworks of asters and goldenrod spilled

silver-smoke-trails of milkweed

WHAT EVERY STREAM KNOWS

how to arrive
without leaving

plunge pool
at the bottom of which
memories are retrieved
the eddy's small
ceremony

the monarch gliding through you
that when you turn to see
is gone

the long current flashing
on and off under the opening
and closing sky

the sudden ache of that
light

luring longing
out of the earth

everyone's secret
hiding place
among reeds and stones

the green heron's poised station

how to alter the path
while keeping the way

PHOTOGRAPH AT EVENING LOOKING
WEST OUT TO SEA

here
woven
into blue grey flying
green white dyes of
streaking sea-sky

and through smooth
soft grey-blue
wash of cantaloupe flushed sky-sea

in this streaming and
stillness at once of
movement and this moment blurring
all the washes of time flashed
streaking silhouettes
wings narrowly
keeling into wind

two seabirds

travelling as if

suspended

heading somewhere

together

and everywhere they have been

and everywhere
they are going

is with them

CHROMATIC CHATTER

tako to ama then
still your octopus
I slide through your eye
and walk across a dry floor
neurons dispersed all the way through

I escape through you
inking my way with these scribbles

I'll take your hand and take you
on a tour of the neighbourhood
where the light is folding
through the shallows

3 hearts – 3 different engines for love
and with all the colours of my arms
how's my reach
I've tasted you

I've repurposed so many things
only my life
seems not to have understood
it's one of them

and each thought of you
acting independently
of the brain
is all possibility

today
my skin sees you

here

in this infinite second
in the crumpled time of thunder
on the sea bed inside us

we might be

thinking magically or
living forever
without even holding
our breath

THERE IS A WAY

                              black-throated clouds
molten-tipped
smoked gold air
                              almost a fragrance
the valley ripe with haze
in late sun
                              scatter-burst
                              of leaf-fall

the voice of shiver disperse
                              circumnavigate jubilato
or tantalize annihilate and sigh all
in the tide of pine
at the top of the hill

I've been waiting
for your mantis your hieroglyph there
your song and your ointment
amid that old history
from the one who flew down the stairs

and became a bird
                              before the closed gate
of the floor
                              rose up
the wave in the stone flowing past

as if the now were a time lapse
filled with afterlives

what we truly know
if even for an instant
we know by heart

and so the world speaks to us

THE MOMENT

the present: time that makes things last through what does not

a moment
sharpens its quill
under my skin

am I remembering
a dream or dreaming
now

hearing things that were
once
familiar differently

through the clarity
of the water
the pike's hovering
by the dock

in a world
where what seemed to matter
no longer does

almost as if
I'm afraid to listen

as if each rivulet returning
to the bay after wavecrash
had streaming back through the shingle
a voice of its own

like love
love's six tasselling anthers
in the world of deep fragrance
that is the trumpet lily

once lost beneath the blah blah blah

as if you'd come out of your life
like a blossom from its sepal
where the hummingbird of the imagination sips

the morning resting
on the upturned palms of leaves

the moment of the lost sentence

the moment they told you you'd failed
that tsunami moment
made out of paper
sunyata
of lightning flicker

the moment of the call
of the missed train

in perpetuity
the call of

the moment
inside the moment

of
there you are

and beyond there

the beyond

FINAL REPORT

in the house of friendly fire they've insisted

you professionalize your hummingbird flight skies

roll out the awkward applause of clouds but they forgot

the virga gown the love affair with shadow and night

even trees ringed with memory have no defence

scalpel scissors
stone paper house of cards a straight flash where the mind
burns down to wink seriously
there are no results look around you there are no results

the real ones we fail to see
and the ones they want you to measure are made up

there is only unfolding a house made of trees or a forest
made of trees or a door
which is an offer of grace

and even as the house collapses in the dust and smoke of
    the word drones
there are still a hundred ways to go through it

SPECTRAL DATA

And though nothing in that dark kingdom is provable,
neither can its nonexistence be proven.

first came the trucks
with their loads of ambiguous objects
that looked maybe at first
like pyramids or thickets of bone

then the floats of clouds
carrying their mixed electrical
signals deep within them

then having lost their guidance
systems the ICBMs
and their interplanetary replacements

and all the extinguished species
their fires out
the houses awash in sand

a line of rimed cedar
from which an asteroid shower
of shadows shoots
streaking north over the
gravitational waves of snow

through which a gang of Vikings are dragging their longboat
containing an amusement park
from the far side of the Rapture

a woman in a cave
blowing ochre onto a wall

and look a Skinner Box
inside of which we have no idea
whose life is being unlearned

and finally the philosophers of language
drawing word balloons in the air

and voila
here we all are

but when does the poem begin
you might ask

and I too wondered

thinking it may have scampered away
up the inside of the wall of the church
I haven't sat in since grade school

some things are just not amenable
not remediable
but this maybe
isn't one of them
if only FOXP2 had something to say to me

I'd be driving a small wedge
into a looping oscillator and then
screening it such that each
moment of spectral data could be
the incipience of a future memory

as if time were a crystal
whose infinitely refractive room you enter
but on whose facets
your reflections continue to glide

and here in timelessness
the piano's percussive ivories
stroked and hammered crisscrossing
through the slanting
evening light
high up in the hayloft

alone

and in the blink of an eye

only needlepoints of sunset

pierce the barn boards

making a sieve

of the darkness

as I lift my fingers from the keys

NOTES AND ACKNOWLEDGMENTS

"after all this time": The line "if the abandoned poem speaks" is from Robert Kroetsch, "Delphi: Commentary," in *Completed Field Notes* (McClelland and Stewart, 1989).

"bent water light something": The epigraph is from Wallace Stevens, "The Snow Man," in *The Collected Poems of Wallace Stevens* (Alfred A. Knopf, 1969).

"commemorative": All phrases are from Ciaran Carson, "Yves Klein, IKB, 1959," in *Still Life* (The Gallery Press, 2019).

"catechism": Some phrases are from Steven Feld, "Aesthetics as Iconicity of Style, or 'Lift-up-over Sounding': Getting into the Kaluli Groove," *Yearbook for Traditional Music* 20 (1988): 74–113; and from Patient M.M. reported in Wilder Penfield, *The Mystery of the Mind: A Critical Study of Consciousness and the Human Brain* (Princeton University Press, 1975), 25.

"chromatic chatter": Some phrases are from Amia Srinivasan, "The Sucker, the Sucker," *London Review of Books* 39, no. 17 (7 September 2017), a review of *Other Minds* by Peter Godfrey-Smith and *The Soul of an Octopus* by Sy Montgomery.

"the moment": The epigraph is from Bruno Latour, *Facing Gaia; Eight Lectures on the New Climate Regime* (Polity, 2017). The lines "once lost beneath the blah blah blah" and "beyond there / the beyond" are from the film *The Great Beauty*, co-written by Paolo Sorrentino and Umberto Contarello and directed by Sorrentino.

"spectral data": The epigraph is from Mary Oliver, "The Bright Eyes of Eleanora: Poe's Dream of Recapturing the Impossible," in *Upstream* (Penguin Random House, 2016).

Some of the poems (sometimes in earlier versions) were first published in *Event* ("Lobelia cardinalis," "so this is what it was like," "I'm talking to you tonight from radio nowhere"); *TNQ* ("bent water light something"); the anthology *Spike* published by Cannonscreek Press ("the raft"); and the League of Canadian Poets' *Poem a Day* ("translations from an unknown language"). I am grateful to the editors.

The "Fortune Teller" poems were initially conceived to potentially be designed such that readers could tear out and fold pages into origami. When g.d. currie, editor at *Scrivener Creative Review*, reached out for a contribution to the Louis Dudek special issue (S1, October 2018), I sent along a couple of early pieces (which however do not appear in the book) and I am extremely grateful they wanted to try one as an insert – and it turned out fabulously. Shoutout for their time, energy, and skill.

Shoutout too to Daniel Bratton and Carol Williams of the Elora Poetry Centre for publishing "nightvision" in their newsletter of July 2021.

Bountiful thanks to Edward Carson for his patience, insight, and friendship over many shared lines and lifetimes.

To George Eliott Clarke, Dennis Cooley, Randy Lundy, and Fred Wah, much thanks.

Thanks too to Allan Hepburn, series editor, and to Kathleen Fraser, managing editor, at McGill-Queen's for helping me with unfinishing *unfinishing*,